A More
Loving World

A More
Loving World

The School of Life

Published in 2022 by The School of Life
First published in the USA in 2022
930 High Road, London, N12 9RT

Cover design by Marcia Mihotich
Typeset by Kerrypress
Printed in Latvia by Livonia Print

A proportion of this book has appeared online at
www.theschooloflife.com/thebookoflife

The School of Life is a resource for helping us understand
ourselves, for improving our relationships, our careers
and our social lives – as well as for helping us find calm
and get more out of our leisure hours. We do this through
creating films, workshops, books, apps and gifts.

www.theschooloflife.com

ISBN 978-1-912891-86-3

10 9 8 7 6 5 4 3 2 1

Contents

I.
A
Loveless
World

We begin with a vast and urgent claim: that we have forgotten how to love; that we are living – and suffering – in a loveless world. We have lost ourselves to intolerance, partisanship, cruelty and paranoia. If civilisation ends, it won't be because we have wrecked the climate or let off nuclear warheads; it will be due primarily to a failure of love. Worse, we have little clue what precisely is ailing us; we lack any sharp sense of the sickness choking us. Almost every agony commonly shelved as an issue of economics or politics is at base the result of a shortfall of love. The furies and horrors that unfold on the public stage are symptoms of our collective distempers of the heart.

We should admit that, without any ill intent, we harbour a narrow and impoverished sense of what love really is. We dwell in a loveless world because we have depleted one of the central words in our emotional lexicon.

Love is not, as we have too often come to believe, the special excitement we feel when in a cosy restaurant in the presence of someone unusually beautiful, pure, clever and accomplished. It is not the thrill of reaching shyly across the table to hold the hand for the first time of a miraculous being in whose eyes we sense a distinct tenderness and capacity to thrill. It is not an exclusive admiration for a favoured person of exceptional virtue. This may be moving and in certain moods important too, but it is not what has the power to redeem civilisation.

The love that counts does not depend on desire or adoration; nor does it focus on an approbation of a single person. Love is first and foremost what we should feel around all the many people it is so tempting to curse and to hate; those whom we instinctively believe are mistaken, ugly, irritating, venal, wrong-headed or ridiculous; those who may have made some truly serious mistakes and offended our moral codes; those who are dismissed by right-thinking opinion and condemned by the mob. To learn to *love* such people is the real accomplishment – and the summit of our humanity.

It is love when we can look at someone who appears misguided, lazy, entitled, angry or proud and, instead of labelling them despicable, can wonder with imagination and sympathy how they might have come to be this way; when we can perceive the lost, vulnerable or hurt child that must lie somewhere within the perplexing or dispiriting adult.

It is love when we can accept that most of the irksome things that others do stem not from 'evil' or an intention to hurt or wound, but from some form of buried, unexplained and unmasterable anxiety or distress; when we can look upon the human race as benighted and confused, very seldom as wicked.

It is a small but telling instance of love when a toddler throws their supper on the floor and screams that their parent is a poo, and instead of striking back, the grown-up picks them up, calms their fury and forgives them – as they have already done a thousand times before (over the crayon on the wall and the broken radio, the rudeness to Granny and the tantrum at nursery) and discovers the energy to wonder what might have provoked their child to be so difficult: perhaps they are tired or teething, feeling at a low ebb or beset by jealousy towards a sibling. This attitude is admirable enough when it unfolds in the home, but it is yet greater and more important when it is directed towards the world at large, towards strangers who don't have especially cute cheeks or sparkling eyes – and who might be staring back from a picture in the newspaper on their way to prison, or on a podium having just won an election representing a political party we abhor.

It is love when we grow our capacities for kindness rather than relying on our naturally occurring amiable impulses. Love means making the effort to extend our compassion beyond the bounds of attraction so that we may look generously on those that some might have deemed beyond the pale or 'undeserving': a category that includes not just the low-paid or immigrants but less familiar targets too, like a disgraced CEO, a badly behaved pop star, a shamed pundit or a right-wing magnate. If we understood love properly, when we said we loved a person, we wouldn't necessarily mean that we admired them or felt a kinship with them, but that we had taken steps to grasp the secret story of how they had come to be the way they are; that we had a handle on all the many difficulties that underpinned their troubling and objectionable sides.

It is love when we accept that the forbearance we ourselves crave, because of how many errors we have made and how foolish we have been, is in fact owed to everyone; when we can apply to others (especially those who are quite unlike us) an idea that feels so plausible in relation to our own flaws: that we can be good people despite having done silly things; that we don't merit condemnation in spite of our unfortunate aspects; that we should not be conflated with our worst moments; that we are still somewhere the little children we once were, crying out for reassurance, comfort, a kindly eye and a second (or a hundredth) chance.

*

All too often, we moralise, castigate, denounce, and punish. We think of ourselves as good people even as we pour contempt on our enemies, indulge our prejudices and blow on the embers of partisanship. We think we are believers in love because we like to go on dinner dates and celebrate wedding anniversaries. But in truth we risk becoming the most dangerous sorts of people: those disinclined to question the ways in which they hate; those a little too convinced of their own virtue; those who suspect it is invariably someone else's fault.

How might have we allowed ourselves to forget the highest promises of love? Four reasons suggest themselves:

One:
The Problem
of Romanticism

The difficulties begin with the way the word 'love' has been co-opted by the most powerful ideology to have emerged in the last 250 years. Beginning in Western Europe in the 18th century and then gradually spreading to all corners of the globe, the movement of ideas known as Romanticism has made us imagine that when we talk of love, we must invariably be speaking of the love of two starstruck individuals revelling in a sense of each other's specialness; that love must always be about the longing we feel in the library or the supermarket, at the public swimming pool or on the boulevard when we glance at a graceful person whom our instincts tell us must be the answer to our loneliness and our desire. Romanticism has insisted – not unfairly – that love is the most powerful experience we are capable of, but it has limited its definition to an erotically infused, admiration-based concern of one person for another; it has equated love with a crush.

In working its effect on our minds, Romanticism has benefited from the assistance of the most talented poets, songwriters, painters, novelists and filmmakers. 'There are some people who would never have fallen in love if they had not heard there was such a thing,' quipped the 17th-century French essayist, François de La Rochefoucauld – and Romanticism has made it impossible not to hear about, and wait upon, this 'thing's' arrival with the keenest anticipation. It has ensured that when they ride a train, dignified people can in all seriousness hope that they might lay eyes on a wondrous creature somewhere in the countryside between two cities who could, at a stroke, turn into the meaning of their life.

Humans have always felt the swoon of erotic desire, but only thanks to Romanticism's bold gambit have entire populations begun to think that such passions might constitute the summit of existence.

There might, in forgotten corners, still be lone voices insisting that this is not the whole story or the most important part of love, but these voices have largely lacked reach, powers of persuasion and

Abraham Solomon, *First Class: The Meeting ... and at First Meeting Loved*, 1854

the right tunes. The task is momentous: to remind ourselves that love matters, but not in the way that we have artfully been serenaded to believe.

Two:
The Problem
of Free Love

Insofar as love has ever broken out of its Romantic veneration of the couple and acquired a more social dimension, in recent times it has involved politics of a very particular sort. Love has been identified with 'free love': with hippies, flower children, bohemians and drop-outs. Love has been a religion espoused by the university-educated offspring of lawyers who dress in colourful robes and chant Eastern mantras.

The tenets of so-called free love have at points been moving and its proponents artistically accomplished; it would take a cynical spirit to deny Janis Joplin or John Lennon their place in the pantheon. But free love has at the same time been unhelpfully self-limiting and unwittingly under-mined its own ideals. It has allowed the concept of love as a political force to attract the suspicion of critical swathes of society: anyone who isn't under 35, who isn't left-wing, who isn't interested in non-monogamy and doesn't want to live in a commune.

Holy Man Jam, Boulder, Colorado, USA, 1970. What it could mean to believe ardently in love; a difficult legacy.

It has alienated the extensive ranks of the house-proud and the timid, of accountants and dentists, of those who can't dance and those who hate parties. Even as it made large and stirring claims about changing the world – about love being the answer to war and pain and a force to save us all – it made an interest in love appear synonymous with naïvety and impracticality, with a nebulous fringe one couldn't trust with the car keys, let alone public spending. It both celebrated love and turned it into an adolescent escapade.

The challenge is to take love seriously, not primarily because doing so would be sweet or kind, provocative or vogueish, but because it would be sensible and cautious, because this is what stern military generals and unidealistic bankers should focus on in their vigilant pursuits of prosperity and safety. Love isn't a drug-assisted halcyon fantasy; it is the most effective security treaty and our finest form of planetary life insurance.

Three:
The Problem
of Christianity

There is one force that has spoken of love with superlative seriousness and the correct kind of depth: Christianity has made love central to its understanding of the destiny and needs of humankind.

It has also advanced a distinctive conception of love: it has argued that it is the essence of love to forgive one's enemies, that we might love a thief or a prostitute, that love-worthiness does not depend on worldly accomplishments, that loving a pauper could be more laudable than paying homage to a king, that to love is to search for the fear and the sorrow beneath the violence and hate of our adversaries and that one should look with charity upon the most apparently abject individuals – who might, at certain moments, include oneself.

The Greeks and the Romans had loved wholeheartedly as well, but they had chosen very different targets for their veneration. They had worshipped strength and beauty, intelligence and

From the classical world to Christianity: the love of Venus (top) to the love of a leper (bottom). Alexandros of Antioch, *Venus de Milo*, c. 130–100 BCE; Cosimo Rosselli, *Sermon on the Mount* [detail], c. 1481–1482.

noble lineage. Their most love-worthy heroes had been Venus and Apollo, paragons of physical and mental virtue respectively. Now Christianity urged us to love vagrants and pus-filled, sore-ridden lepers. It was the first ideological movement in the history of humanity to place prostitutes and disabled people above military leaders and royalty.

Christianity imbued its messages with an unparalleled degree of aesthetic charm and resonance. It employed the finest craftspeople and artists to raise cathedrals in honour of forgiveness, to write cantatas to ritualise clemency and to paint canvases to make palpable the glory of fraternity.

The difficulty for love is that Christianity has been far too successful. Over the centuries, it has monopolised our understanding of what love might involve, turning the notion towards its own particular ends. It has connected up a range of hugely sensible and universal ideas about being charitable, forgiving, kindly and imaginative to a specific story about the sacrifice and heavenly ascent of a supernatural being in the hills of Judea in the mid-Roman period. It has made a specific sort of

Balthasar van Cortbemde, *The Good Samaritan*, 1647

love feel intrinsic to the Christian story rather than belonging to the heritage of all humankind.

Consequently, as Christianity came under pressure from secular forces in the 19th century, as the churches emptied out and faith abated, the love heralded from the pulpits acquired a reactionary aura, tainted by association with ever-more marginalised and implausible doctrines. Talk of brotherly love and compassion acquired the musty and occult smells of the vestry. Exultations of love felt akin to superstition – or, more plainly, witchcraft.

We should respect Christianity's contribution to love without needing to remain forever under the spell of the faith itself. Christianity did not begin humanity's thinking around love; nor can it lay claim to it for eternity. Christianity has been a grand and distinguished host for ideas that are the currency of our species as a whole. There is in reality no necessary connection between love and parables of lepers and Samaritans; these fine tales have been carriers of doctrines that, for our own good, might respectfully jump ship and seek to continue their journeys on more persuasive alternative contemporary vessels.

Four:
The Problem
of Justice

For many of those who are now most ardently intent on creating a better world, what has replaced the Christian-inspired emphasis on forgiveness and brotherly love is the pursuit of something that feels a great deal more objective, hard-edged and rational: *justice*.

Rather than holding on to sentimental ideas of kindness and empathy, the pursuers of justice have been interested in fairness; they have used the clinical instruments of the law and the forces of public outrage to try to ensure that everyone is finally accorded what they actually deserve.

In the name of justice, it has been decreed that certain sections of society should urgently be given a lot more money and access to better jobs, while others should be stripped of their privileges, ridiculed or thrown into jail. Justice calls for a slide rule of worthiness to be passed over each of our names in order that we can be raised or damned.

No element of a person should be ignored in this reckoning: something we did ten or thirty years ago can decide what we are owed into perpetuity. No misdeed, however minor, should be overlooked. There can be no room for quick apologies or forgiveness, for that would mean attempting to wipe out wrongdoing, which would be an insult to all victims. Even the dead should not escape the full glare of justice.

The pursuit of justice sounds reasonable – until one comes face to face with an uncomfortable fact: that if we all ended up with what we truly 'deserved', the world would soon be rendered entirely unliveable. Each of us is such a confusing welter of the good and the bad, the meritorious and the blameable, the admirable and the repulsive that were we to weigh up every soul and throw into the nearest river anyone whose record was not unimpeachably pure, our waterways would quickly become impassable.

There are ways in which we can hope to generate more meritocratic societies: we can adjust educational systems, tax codes and criminal laws. We can tweak reputations and explore how honours are distributed. But after every effort in this direction has been made, we still need to recognise that we will never create a world that is perfectly just. There is far too much 'undeservingness' in each of us; the accidents of fortune are too many, our motives are too hard to discern, the connection between intentions and results are too unstable, we are too often both victims and perpetrators. No one is pure.

Moreover, the attempt to pursue justice at all costs, and the belief that doing so is theoretically possible, has a habit of giving rise to appalling intolerance, for if one really believes that one can be a flawless instrument of righteousness, then there is logically no limit to the degree of rage or the sternness of punishments that can be brought to bear upon 'wrongdoers'.

To speak of love is not to wish that abusers might have free rein or misdeeds flourish; it is to insist that alongside sensible efforts in the direction of justice, we must have equal – or greater – efforts in the direction of tenderness, forgiveness, atonement and imagination. Our goal should not be to create a world in which everyone gets exactly what they *deserve*; it is to try to ensure that as many of us as possible get what we *need*: a different and much more tolerable ambition.

Applied to children, concepts of justice quickly reveal their absurdities. If parents were to give their children exactly what they 'deserved', most small people would at a stroke be put out on hillsides to die, given how ill-tempered, pig-headed and wilful they mostly are. But loving parents don't think this way: they wonder where awkward behaviour comes from, they know how much the child needs to be understood and given opportunities for redemption, they don't allow yesterday's tantrum to arbitrate everything about today's treats; they don't hold grudges.

Whatever the superficial differences between ourselves and 3-year-olds, in this context we are not much different in what we need from others. We don't require yet more strict judges; we need loving parents. We need a chance to say sorry and to be allowed to move on; we need not to be forever identified with our gravest mistakes.

The pursuit of justice may spring from the noblest of motives, but it is a quick route to an unloving hell.

*

These four forces help to explain the erosion of love in our societies. But there is no reason why they should continue to shape the future. We have the opportunity to generate the more loving world we deserve.

II.
Attitudes
That
Foster
Love

We are
all children

Perhaps the finest way to foster a loving attitude towards others is to recall, in the face of difficulty and noxiousness, when we are met with reprehensible or maddening behaviour, that we are in the end all children.

The claim is an odd one. Adults are clearly not children. They have powers of reasoning that quite outstrip those of younger people; they have options and a sound grasp of right and wrong; they are capable of causing serious damage; they should know better. We have every right to lose our temper with them and, where necessary, to lock them up for a long time without compunction. We are tough with adults because we know that they have moral agency. If they have done wrong, if they have offended us, if they have lied or hurt, they had a capacity to do better, which they ignored at their reasonable peril.

Children, on the other hand, are well known for their powers to melt our hearts. Partly this has to do with their physical appearance: with their large eyes, their full cheeks, their unthreatening statures, their tiny, fat, fleshy fingers. Their manner, too, is winning: their habit of mispronouncing words, their way of talking to themselves, their relationship with their soft toys, their fascination with unusual but distinctive small corners of the world (with buttons and brick walls, with our glasses and the cat's tail).

So powerful is their capacity to win us over, we might find it impossible to hate any child whatsoever – a daunting thought in the case of some of the world's more egregious future adults.

Children's power to elicit love can't just be due to their powerlessness, dependence and sweet appearance. The matter is more solidly grounded in psychology. Children attract our tenderness because, when they act in 'bad' or tricky ways, it tends to be easy to work out why they have done so. We can – far more than in the case of adults – discern a path that leads from benevolence and good humour to viciousness and rage. It isn't just that children do less wrong than adults, it's that we can work out why they have done so. They hit their little sister because

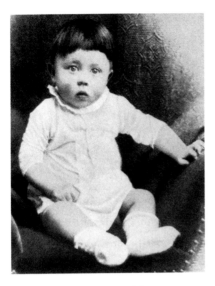

Adolf, aged 9 months, c. 1890

they were feeling left out; they started to steal things from other children because their parents were going through a divorce; they ran away from the party without saying goodbye because they were panicked by a sense of unworthiness.

Overall, when it comes to the psychology of children, we discover a surprising and gentle truth: that 'badness' and difficulty are invariably the result of some form of pain. The child does not start by being dreadful, they become so in response to injury, fear or sorrow. It isn't that the child is by nature an angel – their character contains innately aggressive elements, it's just that these first have to be mobilised by negative external forces.

To argue that this benevolent principle might apply to adults as well as children is a challenging proposal for many of us. When confronted by nasty or terrible behaviour, our thoughts, for understandable reasons, do not generally turn to imagining why it might have occurred. We are too taken up with the injury we have witnessed or sustained to start a psychological investigation. Our minds are dominated by the extreme thoughtlessness of our opponents. We are in no mood to wonder why things came to be as they are. We're satisfied with nimble and compressed reasons: because they're an arsehole; because they're crazy. This will do for now.

Furthermore, investigating the psychology of wrongdoers threatens to undermine any efforts to stop them from doing something awful again. We need to focus on getting bad people fined, reporting them to the police, shaming them publicly, firing them or sending them to prison. Nothing should get in the way of blocking people's capacities to inflict further harm.

Yet it is always open to us to wonder why someone acted as they did – and here we are liable to stumble on a provocative and revolutionary idea: *the reason why little children and adults do wrong is – despite the differences in age and size – exactly the same.* One may be no bigger than a chair, the other can be gigantic and able to carry guns, post lengthy screeds online or start and bankrupt companies, but in the end, the psychology of blunder, meanness and anger is always the same: *evil is a consequence of injury.* The adult did not start off evil, their difficult sides were not hardwired from the start, they grew towards malice on account of some form of wound waiting to be discovered.

It is the work of extraordinary patience and humanity – it is the work of love – to go in search of what these wounds might be. To search is morally frightening because we too easily imagine that it might require us to wind up thinking well of behaviour we know is abhorrent. It doesn't at all: we can remain appalled while simultaneously tracing a path back to the true catalytic factors. The work can also be practically frightening because we imagine that it might require us to leave someone at liberty to cause us or others yet more pain: but again, we can keep the wrongdoer safely behind very high bars even as we sensitively explore the origins of their violations.

Once the full stories of our trespassers become known, our perspective may swiftly rework itself. The bully who pursued us online had once worked as a porter, then been fired some years back and fallen into depression and was facing the bankruptcy courts. The angry populist politician was remorselessly belittled by a powerful father. The sexually impulsive person used their addiction to calm themselves down from some unmasterable anxieties related to early emotional neglect. Our judgement on behaviour never has to change, but our sense of why it occurred can be transformed.

The discipline of psychotherapy has been central in helping us to chart the sometimes unobvious or contrary connections between a symptom and its genesis. Boastfulness may have its roots in fear; anger can mask terror; hatred can be a defence against love. A haughty air can take hold as a way of compensating for invisibility. A satirical manner can be a shield against an exiled longing for sweetness. Most of the time, psychotherapy assists the victims of injury to overcome their traumas; it can accede to a yet more complex and morally subtle mission when it helps us to see more deeply into the minds of those it is easy to dismiss as monsters.

Human beings have not always thought well of small children. For most of history, misbehaviour was punished with a firm hand. Children who stole or told lies were sent to their rooms or hit with a belt. It took us a long time to be able to trust that there must always be a secret agony behind a withheld truth or a theft.

We now realise that not only is it kinder to enquire after such agonies, it is also a great deal more effective. If the goal is to educate children towards goodness and sweetness, a belt isn't the optimal tool. We reform people by showing generosity towards the suffering that accounts for their so-called sins. As we keep forgetting, no one ever becomes kinder through being bullied or publicly shamed. Mockery is not a good instrument for reform. People do not change when they are shouted at; they improve when they are given enough love and security to dare to confront their own failings.

The penal system in most nations has learnt half this story. It will tend to place people below the age of 18 in separate young offenders' institutions, which aim to treat inmates with a degree of kindness and hope – in order to delve into the psychology of transgression with a view to understanding and overcoming its causes. But after this age, for the most part, prisoners are locked up in bare cells and the key is – metaphorically – thrown away. They should have known better, after all.

Yet we are all young offenders, as it were, however old we might actually be; we all need our crimes – no matter how small they may be – to be treated with a degree of sympathy and empathetic investigation. It is no particular achievement to be furious with problematic people and to call them freaks and fools; it is an exquisite feat of mind to be able to imagine them as still, at some level, infants in the cradle.

We are powerful enough to damage others

One of the reasons why we may end up acting more destructively and cruelly than we should is that it can take us a long time to fathom how someone like us could cause trouble for anyone. By 'someone like us', we mean someone who is as unpowerful, as put upon, as much subject to the whims of others, as obscure and forgotten as we generally feel ourselves to be. We know that certain people can be dangerous: those who run corporations, for example, or the heads of governments or investors in oil companies (we might get incensed when we think of what these mighty sorts get up to). It's just that we're nothing like this. We're ordinary; we're not in the midst of history; we're not privileged; we're the victims.

This sense of innocence tends to take hold when we are very young. At that time, it is obvious that we are not qualified to do much damage at all. We are weak before the world and it is always more likely that someone else will be the aggressor.

Parents make unfair demands on us; teachers bully us; strangers might interfere with us.

From this, we may continue to trust in our own inability to aggrieve others. We therefore don't try hard to reassure other people that we like them and that they are of value: why would they need to hear such messages from someone like us? We don't rush to tell our hosts that their hospitality was satisfying; they surely know it anyway. We don't feel we should pay someone a compliment; they obviously have more important friends than us to take care of their self-esteem. If we're feeling oppressed and angry, we might sit down at our computer and lash out at a famous person online: it clearly can't matter to them; they wouldn't be listening to a character as negligible as we are. And thereby, bit by bit, on the back of touching feelings of innocence and powerlessness, we end up adding more than our fair share of poison to the collective bloodstream.

To be a loving person is to wrestle with a profoundly improbable idea: that however modest our position in society might be, however much we may have been maltreated in the past, however mesmerised we are by the deplorable behaviour of powerful individuals, however shy and frail we are, we are constantly capable of causing other people significant hurt.

Loving people understand the extreme psychological susceptibility of everyone who crosses their path. They might have a neighbour, someone who is much more successful than they are and who holidays abroad several times a year, whom they still take care to share a few warm words with in the morning, knowing how a blank stare can hurt even someone who goes paragliding in the summer and has an elegant car. Even though one of their old friends is now a professional chef and seems confident about their work, the loving guest nevertheless bothers to write a witty and careful few lines of thanks after a dinner. There may be a big gap in age or status between them and their boss, but that doesn't mean that they won't say something encouraging when this figure has to go into hospital for a routine operation.

The loving know that you can be employed at the dry-cleaner's or work as an attendant at a cinema and still play a role in someone's life through a small act of graciousness and solicitude. At the same time, they are aware that you could leave an unkind comment online – just a few words reminding a celebrity living thousands of miles away that they're a piece of shit – and thereby help to strip away one of the last reasons why someone might bother to keep living.

The loving know how much everyone suffers from feelings of self-doubt, worthlessness, loneliness and pain beneath a veneer of imperviousness and strength. They may not have the precise details to hand, but they grasp enough about the general picture: how much each one of us is haunted by self-recriminations, how weighed down we are by opportunities we have missed, how isolated and overlooked we feel.

The loving intuit that there is a large gap between what people will tell us of their difficulties and what is almost certainly going on inside them. The conditions of society require a great deal of surface bravery; it is easy to miss the desperation. The loving have their senses open: they look out for signs of pain, they don't wait to be overwhelmed by evidence. They know about pride and our reluctance to let people in on our defeats. They know how much we collude in keeping people at bay, even as we long for comfort. That's why the loving write so many thank you notes, make so many apparently routine phone calls to say hello and leave openings in their conversations where others might venture a confession or a question. They aren't being fake or putting on airs; they're keeping the agony involved in being human at the forefront of their minds.

At a collective level, we describe the heightened awareness of our susceptibility to insult and harm as 'manners'. History shows how long it has taken humanity to acquire manners in different areas. It now seems natural that we should ideally express gratitude to those who offer us gifts, shouldn't eat with our fingers, should avoid burping loudly and mustn't spit in the faces of those who irritate us – but the historical record tells another tale. What we might take to be 'normal' impulses to be modest, restrained and thoughtful are the hard-won fruits of a long and unsteady civilising process. We've only been using forks since Catherine de' Medici promoted their use in the 1550s; we've only been writing thank you letters since the royal courts of Europe spread the habit in the 18th century. For the largest part of our presence on the earth, it has been customary to behead our enemies, to defecate in front of strangers and to use derogatory words towards the inhabitants of other lands.

Manners can seem irritatingly artificial and untrue to who we 'really are', but the loving know that it is no treat for anyone to be exposed to the full and unvarnished reality of another person. They are kind enough to shield everyone they encounter from an authenticity that is likely to include large reserves of irritability, unfairness, prejudice and self-pity. The loving don't feel any need to take other people fully into the darkness of their hearts; they don't need to be honest at any cost; they know that sincere kindness may mean leaving a huge amount unexpressed.

Though it may seem as if we now have all the manners we could possibly need, the loving also recognise how much further there is to go. We are only at the dawn of understanding how destructive an online comment might be; the power of the media to shame us is barely grasped, and generally discovered by individuals only when it is far too late. Our loud, self-promoting, angry, justificatory way of life exacts an unexplored and devastating toll on our psyches.

Small children do us a great favour by tending to burst into tears when they are in pain. Adults who look after small ones for the first time may be surprised by how delicate their feelings are: they only raised their voice slightly and now the 3-year-old is in floods of tears; it was only a passing sarcastic joke, and now the little one is terrified or sulking under a blanket.

We shouldn't wonder at this tenderness of heart; it belongs to all of us once we are properly attuned to our sensitivities. Our lives are constantly demeaned by missing small acts of grace: by the reassurance that doesn't come, by the viciousness that isn't held back, by the comfort that isn't accorded. The loving never let this fragility out of their sight. It doesn't matter that they might apparently be bit-part actors in the dramas of the world, they know that they wield a potentially decisive power to redeem or to damn, to depress or to cheer. They appreciate that they may be the last stop between a stranger and a decision to end it all. They don't wait for obvious cries of help; they know that the emergency of being alive is general and ongoing.

The difference between loving and being loved

The world is a lot less thoughtful and kind than it might be because of a widespread failure to explore with sufficient vigour a generally submerged distinction between 'loving' and 'being loved'.

We tend to learn about 'being loved' first. If things go right, in our earliest days, with miraculous-seeming efficiency and regularity, someone is on hand to bring us milk, to open the curtains, to take us to the park, to put on our socks, to gently wash our limbs. When we can't take it anymore and start to scream, they take us firmly in their arms and stroke our soft hair. When we are bored, they entertain us by putting us on their back for a ride around the garden. When it's our birthday, they conjure up a cake and a crowd of well-wishers. When our room is chaotic, they get on their knees and tidy up the clothes and toys. When our buttons break, they sew on some new ones from a box with flowers on the lid that they keep for the occasion. When we realise on the school steps that we've forgotten our gym shoes, they drive home to pick them up.

As we reach adulthood and think of falling in love with another person outside the family, it is natural to imagine a continuation of this kind of careful ministry and attentiveness. We picture someone who will place us at the centre of their universe, who can listen to our woes, who can save us from isolation and can reassure us of our potential and our rightness.

It may therefore be confusing and wounding when we begin to have relationships and discover that, outside of a brief initial period of intense enthusiasm, the love we taste may be relatively ambivalent. Despite talk of loving us, a partner may at times be ill-tempered, personally preoccupied, unwilling to entertain us, slow to deliver comfort and intermittent in some of their attentions. It feels natural to blame this person for not understanding the real nature of love and, despite their protestations, we might separate in order to go in search of more ardent and credible figures.

But our quest is likely to be frustrated so long as we fail to recognise that the love we enjoyed in childhood was a masked and heavily edited variety that we cannot hope to rediscover outside of the specific confines of our families. Out of immense thoughtfulness, we were at first shielded from the sharper edges of the distinction between 'loving' and 'being loved'. Our caregiver did not let us in on the full price exacted by the need to look after us. They did not show us their tears when, after another day of tending to our appetites and ideas, they retired to their room and sobbed from tiredness and regret for all that they had had to sacrifice to ensure us a reassuring start in life. They did not reveal their boredom at having to read – for the fourth time – a story that we found hilarious. They did not hint that they didn't speak to us about their own feelings for fear of boring or intimidating us. They did not tell us that, as they gave us piggy backs and pointed out the squirrels on the upper branches of the oak tree in the garden, they were beset by near-hysterical worries about a project at work. We knew them only as devoted, thoughtful, alert, balanced, entirely focused on us and profoundly committed to our welfare.

This is a heroic effort that fortifies us for adulthood, but it can also store up trouble for us. It may mean that we spend years failing to understand that the love we once knew was a one-way, time-limited gift that we cannot recreate in the more mutual circumstances of grown-up life. We may be slow to take on board that maturity requires us to do something unfamiliar: to *give* rather than to wait to *receive* love. We may have to laugh when we are weary, hold back when it would be easier to lash out, act patiently when our impulse is to lose our temper and put up with awkward or tedious behaviour that tries us. We may have to see a lot of friends we find superficial or threatening. We may have to hold our tongue. We may need to be unhappy for a time. We may have to be, in rotating shifts, the 'parent' to the other's panicked and bewildered child. Furthermore, we need to enter a frame of mind in which our efforts feel normal to us, rather than a betrayal or an aberration. That we are sometimes uncared for, that our needs may take a back seat, that attention is at some moments disproportionately not on us: these are not signs that true love has failed, but that it has begun.

Love is not simply the warm emotion of finding ourselves on the receiving end of someone else's hard work. It is the willingness to devote ourselves to the welfare of other humans, even as this mocks many of our first choices and inclinations. The world will become a more loving place when we can more regularly master our offended, impulsive, furious aspects in the name of other people; when more of us can bear the sacrifices of being grown-ups.

We all
need charity

We tend to associate the word 'charity' with the gifting of material goods to the less advantaged and – in the prosperous world at least – with the problems of somebody else. We admire charity; we tend never to expect to be its direct recipients.

The stories of charity that come down to us through the Catholic tradition exult those who were especially selfless in their ministry to the poor. There was St Nicholas, who rescued prostitutes; St Francis of Assisi, the son of a prosperous silk merchant, who put aside a promising mercantile career to devote his life to the starving and the homeless; St Vincent de Paul, who attended to the needs of freed slaves; St Elizabeth Ann Seton, who founded schools for disadvantaged girls.

Such examples have shaped our sense of what charity involves, but they have also subtly limited our understanding of what this crucial word might mean to us. In its fundamental sense, to receive charity has little to do with money; it simply means being gifted something that we need but cannot secure for ourselves. Historically and overwhelmingly, this may have involved an income, but in reality our requirement for charity extends far beyond this.

However buoyant our finances, we all require what might be termed psychological charity. No life can proceed far without moments of crisis when we are thrown back on the imagination and sympathy of others, when we can't bargain with the world on our own terms, and when we are, as it were, on our knees, asking people we depend upon to consider our case with greater compassion than the law or prevailing opinion might allow. We can all easily be described in brief and humiliating terms, as 'monsters', 'weirdos' or 'losers'. Charity works in another direction; it involves the energy to hold on to a sense of us as properly human, despite our failings. The charitable person looks beneath the surface to locate the complicated, stricken soul within the off-putting shell.

Perhaps we have done something deeply silly at work. Or we have lost our temper with a friend. Or we have been on an injudicious escapade. Or we have acted in our relationship in a way that means our lover would have every right to throw us out. As a result, we'll be – metaphorically or truly – in the begging position.

At such moments it would be easy for those whom we are beseeching to sigh, turn away and sourly remark that we should have known better. But those who understand love will grasp how easy it is for us to let our worst impulses overwhelm us, how compelled we can all occasionally be in directions that don't reflect our full intelligence or sensitivity. They know about the universal effects of tiredness, lust and greed; they have personal experience of vanity, immaturity and envy. They know how comingled the good and the bad are in themselves and in each of us in turn.

Here the promoters of psychological charity have a slender advantage over those who attempt to turn us towards material charity. Many of us will never have to ask anyone for our next meal or for a blanket – and we implicitly know this. Our imperviousness to extreme poverty renders us, in small but perceptible ways, hard towards those characters who approach us with a cup in hand; they may be weeping, but they aren't anyone we will resemble any time soon.

However, we can never assume that we will live out our days without having to cry out, on a repeated basis, for high degrees of psychological charity from the people around us. Sooner or later, we will run into problems – almost certainly of our own making – that will provide a harsh audience with all the excuses they need to throw us to the wolves.

With any luck, we'll also be able to call on someone who knows a little about love; someone who has learnt how often they themselves have strayed from the virtuous path, and therefore is in no mood to cast aspersions on the worthiness of those who are asking them for mercy in turn. Right now, we may have a good name, a satisfying career and a kind family. Yet none of our advantages are solid, as the loving can't forget; we are all only ever a few small steps away from being shamed and abandoned, desperate and mocked. To be a loving person is to know that charity isn't a passing, guilt-coated duty towards those who haven't managed to get a job; it is a universal requirement for the sort of kindness and thoughtfulness that we have never strictly earned, but won't survive without.

We are
not pure

There is a paradox at the heart of what it means to be a loving person. On the one hand, the aspiration would seem to necessitate that we be as 'good' as possible. On the other, those who feel that they are very good, who consider their record as spotless and their actions as blameless, can end up exhibiting a rigidity and sternness of heart that may veer into self-righteousness and a distinct sort of cruelty. We have to conclude that truly good people never feel beyond reproach; they know how much is crooked and unfortunate in their souls and on this basis go easy on the transgressions of others. They are properly kind because they never feel very pure themselves.

For most people, the moment of maximal perceived purity tends to be in late adolescence, a phase that for many of us, psychologically speaking, can continue deep into middle age. We awaken from the fog of childhood to acquire a newly robust impression of moral clarity. We see for the first time how bad people really are, and grow determined to call out evil deeds that we feel we have ignored for too long. The teachers are, as we are now able to see, mostly only in it for themselves, the government is filled with time-wasters and egoists, corporations only want to protect their own interests, and closer to home, our parents are nauseatingly compromised, sentimental, selfish and variously lustful or weak-willed.

These lapses outrage our sense of right and wrong and fire a crusading spirit. It seems beyond belief that certain people who need to be exposed and expunged could be quite so venal in their actions: why would a respectable company not do more to help the forests and the seas? Why would a politician care so much about narrow party interests? Why would someone break up a family because of a passing infatuation? Why would an adult lose their temper over minor details? Why would a person get involved in the status race and worry so much about their earnings or how big their house was?

Adolescent minds can be particularly exercised by the idea that valuable things might have murky and muddled origins. In response, they will be in no mood to make excuses. If the talented painter behaved badly at home, then their work should be taken down from galleries and museums. If the benefactor turned out to harbour racist views, they should be stripped of their honours and made to disappear from history.

The adolescent is able to be so outraged because the flaws that drive unfortunate behaviour are so unknown to them from the inside. They have never yet felt the pull between duty and desire. They haven't experienced the temptations of power. They haven't been inducted into how desperate one may grow after years in a relationship. They haven't been under the sort of professional pressure that means one can end up shouting intemperately even at people one loves. They haven't witnessed the slow death of many of their dreams or the onset of unmasterable moods of indolence and self-hatred. They haven't known from close up the agony that can ensue when friends succeed – and our own professional stagnation is thrown into relief.

It may take a while until life's appalling complexity hits the adolescent mind; until they notice that, in spite of all their worthiness, they have in certain areas acted with some of the very malevolence they have hitherto located only in other people: the fraudulent CEO, the degenerate politician, their unpleasant father. They may have judged many people with steely implacability before they find themselves falling in love with one person even while they are pledged to another, before they act unreasonably with their own child, before they are dragged down by moods of despair and sadness they cannot get past, before they feel so weak and ignored inside that they start to boast and buy goods that they can't afford in the hope of being noticed and admired.

They may be greying by the time someone whose good opinion they crave turns around and, with cold-hearted fury, accuses them of having been a 'selfish, ungrateful idiot' and they are made to recognise that they truly have been such a thing – despite being, in so many other ways, kind and humane, thoughtful and courteous, committed to protecting the environment and enlightened in their attitudes to redistributive taxes. At last, the former adolescent is ready to take on board the agonies of adulthood and to be appropriately kind in response.

We have to learn how corrupt we are, how insipid we can be, how little we understand, in order to be in any position to bestow adequate warmth on our fellow humans. We will be ready to love when we have absorbed the full extent of our capacity to be bad.

Unfamiliar targets
of love

Attempts to render us more loving tend to try to focus our minds on those people that, in the ordinary course of things, we are prone to step over without the slightest thought or feeling of guilt.

Historically, this has tended to mean one category above all: the poor. In most societies since the dawn of time, the materially underprivileged have received opprobrium and neglect. They have been left to starve outside of the city gates; they have been kicked and abused by guards; they have been splattered with mud by the passing gilded carriages of aristocrats.

It was the accomplishment of Christianity in the West and Buddhism in the East to speak with special generosity about this ignored category. Thanks to parables and songs, sermons and exhortations, societies' empathetic powers were opened up to the needs of the unemployed and the hungry, the homeless and the destitute. It was the feat of these religions to nudge well-housed people into thinking about vagrants in alleyways, to prompt princes to clean the feet of paupers and to so needle the consciences of the mighty that they would endow schools and alms-houses.

However imperfect the results may be, we can't doubt the sizeable victory of the initiative. Our education in empathy has been so thorough, when we hear talk of needing to exhibit greater love outside of a Romantic context, our minds tend immediately to picture those who are deprived of material resources. Yet if we become forensic about the word 'love' and return to first principles, what it really means to be a loving person is to be prepared to extend sympathy to all unfamiliar targets – all those whom a heedless world is used to mocking and cursing, judging and sidelining. It is the unfamiliarity that is essential and ethically admirable – but quite who happens to be an unfamiliar target will shift along with changes in public awareness and sensibility.

As we look at the contemporary world and wonder who might especially deserve love, we may, with a proper understanding of the word 'love' in mind, come to a few surprising conclusions. The hungry and the homeless are worthy recipients, of course, but other proper objects of love might include powerful politicians who have lost elections and face the ridicule of the media, well-remunerated industrialists who have been fired from their jobs after a sudden dip in the share price, famous actors who have been caught up in scandals and blacklisted, or acclaimed singers who have fallen into mania under the pressures of fame. We might need to direct love to the right-wing newspaper magnate who is a favourite figure of hate in progressive circles.

By saying that we need to 'love' such people, we don't, crucially, mean that we should approve of them or think them admirable, or give them whatever they ask for. What we mean is that we should, under the aegis of love, be ready to accord them imagination, a lack of vindictiveness and a rare degree of sympathy; that we should be ready to look beneath the obvious externals, the bluster and the arrogance, the unfortunate manner and the privileged contempt in search of the damaged, lost and confused child within. Despite every encouragement to disparage and curse, we might delve with enlightened interest into what might have moulded a particular human into their present challenging form. Against the headwinds of public opinion, we might exchange anger and righteousness for curiosity.

It must have taken immense bravery in early Christian times to invite a pauper into one's house for dinner or to make a speech in a palace in praise of the integrity of prostitutes. These were deeply unfamiliar targets of love. No one had ever before spoken of loving someone with leprosy; there had never been sermons in temples in honour of those who couldn't afford to buy a pair of shoes.

We can be equally surprising in our choices of whom to love today. We should be challenged to show love towards whomever it has grown typical to mock. Our societies may be big on empathy, but they remain awkwardly limited in their sense of where its warming spotlight should fall. And yet the essence of love is to defy all stereotypes of worthiness. Wherever it would be simple, customary and respectable to hate, precisely there is where we should love.

The origins
of 'sin'

Traditionally, Christianity identified seven 'deadly sins': failings of character that were to be particularly condemned by the Church and avoided by all righteous people: pride, envy, wrath, gluttony, lust, sloth and greed.

We may not use precisely such theological words today, and we may not imagine the Creator of the universe as someone who organises chastisement for people for their lapses. But, in the spirit in which we interpret failings of character in the online and real worlds, we tend to exhibit an austere and ungenerous set of attitudes that can – to those on the receiving end – feel on par with the worst moments of the Inquisition.

We may believe that, through our harshness, we are helping humanity to improve, but if moral development is our goal, then it pays to try to understand what truly drives people in their most regrettable acts.

We stand to stumble on a surprising truth: behaviour that we call bad is never simply that. It represents an unfortunate first response to difficulty and distress that could, if it were properly understood, guided and forgiven, be redirected towards nobler ends. We aren't evil so much as in a lot of pain in a number of areas.

Let's consider each of the seven sins in turn:

Pride

It can seem as if we end up boasting and grandstanding because we're so pleased with ourselves. But boasting is only ever a symptom of an underlying sense of invisibility. We so badly need to promote an idea of our own importance as behind the scenes our very right to exist feels in doubt. This is why, of all people, the proud don't need to be abruptly reminded of their terribleness; this is precisely what they secretly know a lot about already. They need encouragement to feel a more genuine pride in their own merits so as not to have to keep lying and blustering in order to impress an imagined critical audience.

Envy

Envy is a graceless way of confronting an idea that is, in other contexts, fundamental to decent ambition as well as modesty of character: the notion that we are incomplete, imperfect and in need of evolution. Envy grows out of the legitimate insight that others have something to teach us, but is spoilt by a degree of inaccuracy and panic about what this might actually be. Ideally, envy should function as our teacher. We should note when it strikes us, sift through its confused signals and use it to work out what we would like to be and do. The solution isn't to be told to stop being envious; it is to be helped to get better at understanding what is missing from our lives in order to do justice to our latent possibilities.

Wrath

The mean and angry things that we say when we're upset are almost never truly meant. They are the result of panic and anxiety. We call someone a stupid fool because we are, at that moment, terrified. We shout because we feel we're fighting for our lives. Instead of being repeatedly told that it's appalling to get angry (we know this quite well already), what we need to soothe us is someone who can demonstrate a proper understanding of our underlying fears; who can reassure us for our fragility, not berate us for our roars.

Gluttony

We eat too many chicken wings and toasted sandwiches not because we're greedy, but because we are deprived of emotional ingredients we can't name or locate. We crave love far more than we want calories, but we don't know how to build up the nourishing connections that would satisfy our souls. The solution isn't to be lectured on the virtues of eating less but to be shown the way towards new sources of kindness and attention. Our excess weight is a sign that we cannot find our way to what we lack deep down.

Lust

We continuously jump into bed with people and scroll through naked images not out of physical desire but because we are lonely. The so-called 'bad' and erotic things we crave feel so exciting because they are a distraction from our suffering and proof of the open-ended affection of which we are in such short supply. Ideally we'd not be less lustful, we'd be clearer about what we genuinely need from sex: acceptance by a kind-hearted person of our messy, complex and profane selves.

Sloth

Our laziness is a form of fear. We can't bear to get down to our work, because if we were to apply ourselves, we risk humiliation; so long as we do not try, there is no possibility of failure. Behind our inaction is a constant anticipation of disaster. We can begin to work only once the fear of doing something badly is finally trumped by a terror of doing nothing at all.

Greed

The powerful urge to take more than our fair share is a reaction to a feeling of deprivation; we've felt so neglected and vulnerable, we need the whole cake and money for twenty lifetimes. Our fears of emptiness are so entrenched, we keep trying to solve a problem that lies in a past we haven't yet been able to confront. To others, we may look advantaged and privileged; inside we are desperate and hollow.

In short, our 'sins' are never signs of being a so-called bad person; they are the shape our unmet needs take when we haven't found (or been effectively helped to find) a better way of addressing our emotional deprivations. We don't need to be berated or threatened with hell. We need a form of open affection that welcomes us as we are; we need forgiveness that doesn't involve criticism and a tenderness that delicately locates our vulnerability without crushing us.

This is what we've always been searching for in vain – via that extra serving of fries, the laziness, the shady deals, the furious outbursts, the vain moments of self-praise and the clandestine erotic rendezvous or hours of internet pornography. These are not sins, as traditionally understood, but attempts, however radically imperfect, to find a way to make peace with our troubled selves.

Our tragic
condition

When it comes to our sense of who does and doesn't deserve punishment, we tend to operate with a simple dichotomy: either someone is guilty, and therefore must pay for their misdeeds, or they are innocent and should be allowed to walk free. Off the back of this divergence, we also know how to apportion our sympathies: the innocent merit our concern, the blameworthy have it coming to them.

And yet when we examine a great many lives from close up, a more troubling reality comes to light. In scenarios we know as 'tragic', the apportioning of blame becomes impossible. A person may have done something quite wrong: they ended a relationship tactlessly, they had an affair, they lost their temper and said words they shouldn't. Their behaviour has clearly earned them some form of comeuppance.

But it's the sheer scale of this eventual comeuppance that can tip due process into tragedy. In certain cases, after an affair has ended tactlessly, the rejected party doesn't merely weep and take their leave; they may seek to destroy their ex's reputation, post untrue allegations online and get them discredited among all potential employers. Or, equally tragically, they may kill themselves – exacting a life-long burden of guilt. Alternatively, a fleeting hot-tempered moment at work one afternoon might mean that someone is hauled before a tribunal, sacked for gross misconduct and can never find another job again, prompting the collapse of their marriage and the destruction of their relationship with their children. There are lives that are undone by a single word or email.

What defines tragedy is the disproportion between offence and punishment. There may be some primary fault: a lapse of reason, a degree of selfishness, an instance of lust or greed. But the toll is appalling and mesmerising in its scale and reach. It was the ancient Greeks who first and best identified this possibility, named it tragic and gave rise to a tradition of writing plays in which one could, at close quarters, follow the disintegration of someone's life from a relatively minor error to disaster, shame and death.

In the works of the great Greek tragedians – Aeschylus, Euripides, Sophocles – we observe intelligent, well-disposed characters who make errors of the sort we are all guilty of but, through the spiteful machinations of fate, have to pay an exceptional price for them. In Euripides' *Medea*, Jason, an adventurer and an ambitious politician, grows bored of his wife, Medea. It is understandable enough: they have two children, the marriage has been lengthy, long relationships can be stifling. Jason finds himself falling in love with the beautiful and younger Glauce, daughter of King Creon; it happens all the time. What Jason does not foresee is Medea's response: so incensed is she by the betrayal, so fragile is her mind, that she exacts revenge in the only way she knows will truly destroy Jason: by ending the lives of their children.

Tragedy is sadly not limited to legendary examples on the stage that we can leave behind after a few hours. The tragic dimension follows us deep into our own lives. We may try to push the possibility far out of consciousness. The media – through which we learn so much about the errors and crimes of our fellow humans – prefers to keep things simple. It regales us with a stream of one-dimensional villains: greedy capitalists, faithless spouses, sexual perverts. It tries to reassure us that harm only comes to the obviously wicked.

We want so badly to believe in such an assurance, but the reality is a good deal more nuanced – and lamentable. When we examine cases from close up, we will discover that the apparently one-dimensionally evil business person we read about in a headline had no wish to destroy their whole company and ruin the livelihoods of thousands. The unfaithful spouse was carried away by momentary desire: the marriage had been barren for a long time, but they weren't trying to drive anyone mad. The so-called pervert was beset by compulsions they regretted the moment they were exhausted. And all the while, these figures maintained sides that were generous, sweet-natured, intelligent and gifted. At the height of their fortunes we would have been proud to know them. And, needless to say, when they were little, they were filled with promise and had gleeful eyes and adorable smiles.

People emphatically do not get what they deserve. We are often short-sighted, selfish, greedy and cruel, but the intensity with which we have to suffer for some of our transgressions observes no reasonable limits. In the early hours, the world's bedrooms are filled with people who both berate themselves for their mistakes and know that the record can never be expunged: the dead cannot be reborn, the relationship cannot be repaired and there will be no other option but to suffer every day of what remains of a doomed life.

We need hearts of stone or simply uncurious minds not to be moved. We would be advised to show some form of loving response for an obvious and self-founded reason: because tragedy is likely to make an appearance in our own lives before too long. There is almost certainly already something that we have done – some oversight we are guilty of, some piece of malice we have perpetrated – that may set in motion a chain of events that could one day result in the destruction of everything we hold dear.

No one has guaranteed us protection from the unequal distribution of punishments; we are the playthings of the gods, and the Greeks did their best to warn us on this score. There can be no reason to continue to cling to naïve models of justice. We have no option but to pity every so-called 'sinner'; we must battle our tragic fates with love.

Be slow
to judge

One of the strangest and most wondrous aspects of
the Christian religion is its emphasis on the
prospect of a Day of Judgement. One day, at the end
of history, when God's design for the earth is at a
close, we are told that the angels will gather the
souls of all those who have ever lived and, in an
area outside the gates of paradise, to the
accompaniment of heavenly music, the sound of
trumpets and the pageantry of lined ranks of saints,
God and his disciples will undertake the careful
appraisal of all our moral natures. Everything we
have ever done and said will be meticulously
calibrated, put onto divine golden scales, judiciously
assessed by an all-seeing, all-knowing, perfect
intelligence – and we will then be accorded what we
truly and actually deserve.

This fanciful tale was not primarily designed to
encourage us to look forward to an actual event,
however pleasing this possibility might be. Far
more wisely and practically, it was employed to
try to staunch our habit of judging and moralising

in the here and now. With a Day of Judgement in store, Christianity sought to stop us trying to do God's work with our own faulty and querulous human instruments.

We are not able to tell what other people are worth. It isn't in our power to decide whether someone is good or bad; we have only faint external signals to go on when determining an individual's merit; we can't peer closely into the relationship between actions and intentions; we can't see clearly into people's pasts, consider every aspect of their childhoods or follow the way their beliefs have developed. We have only headlines and gossip to guide us – and these cannot ever be enough to deliver real justice.

Because we can never arrive at such justice, we should not try to judge at all. As truly loving people, we should let our judgements hover, be constantly reminded that we cannot properly understand what is going on, and be slow to deliver verdicts. The so-called monster may indeed be corrupt, but we can't tell what is at play from our vantage point. How can we possibly know what is in the mind of an apparent deviant? On what basis do we have a right to deliver a judgement on the fate of an errant spouse or a bankrupt tycoon?

While we wait for God and his angels to do their work, the element that must fill the gap in our knowledge is love. Of course, there (probably) won't ever be an actual Day of Judgement. But what there is before us at the breaking of every new dawn is the possibility – far more edifying and more morally elevated still – of a Day of Non-Judgement; another day when we remember that we don't have the full set of facts and that we can't tell what someone has been through; a day when we are committed to resisting swift and callous arbitration; a day when we do not judge because we have learnt to love.

Imaginative
focus

In 1821, the 45-year-old English painter John Constable went out on to Hampstead Heath and did something very loving. He set up his easel and looked closely at an elm tree. He observed the weathering across its bark, the lichen around its base, the moss clinging to its roots; he looked at the water stains that ran down its sides, its canopy of toothed celadon-green leaves and its purple-black buds. He spent around forty hours over a few weeks lavishing attention on an object to which most of us have never accorded more than a minute. Commenting on this capacity after his death, Constable's friend and biographer, Charles Robert Leslie, remarked: 'I have seen him admire a fine tree with an ecstasy of delight like that with which he would catch up a beautiful child in his arms'.

Constable's move feels central to the definition of love because when we consider someone through the eyes of love (it might be a cherubic child or a criminal, a homeless person or a derided celebrity), what we are first and foremost doing is studying

John Constable, *Study of the Trunk of an Elm Tree*, c. 1821

them closely, solicitously and with benevolence. For once, we are enquiring what might actually be motivating them, what they might have been through and the distinctive forces that have shaped them, as particular as the patterns on bark.

The close studies of painters are touching because we recognise in them a degree of care from which we have been exiled in the ordinary run of life. We unconsciously sense how much we secretly long for steady attention to be brought to bear on the world's trees and flowers, domestic scenes and vistas, people and ideas. It may have been a very long time – perhaps early childhood – since someone took a proper interest in details about us: sincerely enquired how we are feeling, looked at each of our fingers, caressed the back of our heads or delved into the nuances of what excites and saddens us. We recognise an attitude of consideration in art by which we are nourished and sustained in life.

Through the eyes of love, we are not crushed into a headline, our case is not dismissed with a rapid ironic sneer, and through thoughtful engrossment, we can expand into our true multi-faceted selves. The early 19th-century Danish painter Johan Thomas Lundbye may have been engaged in drawing flowers, but he was at the same time modelling for us how we might behave when someone comes to tell us that they are getting divorced, or when a child has destroyed their

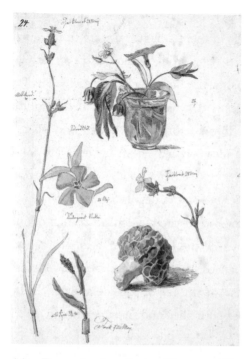

Johan Thomas Lundbye, *Study of Flowers and Plants*, 1840

room in anger, or when we read about the trial and imprisonment of a stranger in the newspaper. We too might follow Lundbye's implicit lesson and take the time to scrutinize every particularity; we might care to see to the underside of things; we might note what is beautiful and tender in inauspicious places.

In 1836, the Austrian painter Jakob Alt allowed us a biographical glimpse into his creative life when he drew his studio in a suburb of Vienna, tracing the objects inside as well as the view onto the mountains of Wienerwald and the houses of the village of Dornbach. The result is a depiction of a place of work, but it is also an inadvertent rendition

Jakob Alt, *View from the Artist's Studio in Alservorstadt toward Dornbach*, 1836

of what it means to love: that is, to look out at the world through the window of our souls with special attention; to open ourselves up to otherness, attempting to give true value to existence; to rescue so-called minor elements from inattention, striving to correct our normal disregard and coldness, and so honouring the true beauty and complexity of things before darkness falls.

III.
Attitudes
That
Hinder
Love

The belief that some people are too 'horrible' to deserve love

Throughout history, certain works of art have tried to teach us to extend our sympathy to strangers by showing how unexpectedly decent they are.

In mid-19th-century France, the painter Jean-François Millet became famous for his tender depictions of the quiet dignity and simple piety of impoverished farm labourers. These were not people with whom the prosperous, educated visitors to elegant art galleries would normally have felt much kinship, but Millet argued that they *deserved* kindness because they were deeply good people despite their unfashionable clothes, lack of money and rustic manners. By highlighting their virtues, he made them easy to love. A similar association is often made today when we are invited to feel sympathy for a devoted school teacher fleeing a war zone or a sweet-looking child struck by a horrible illness.

This is a civilised strategy for bringing more people into the orbit of our good will. But it may

Jean-François Millet, *The Angelus*, 1857–1859

additionally suggest that there are people who properly fall *outside* the range of our sympathy: people who are boastful, vulgar, vain, greedy, mean or corrupt; people who lie without shame, or who are proud of being selfish. If some people *deserve* our love, then (logically) there can be people who *don't*. And indeed, to express sympathy or good will towards them would, in certain circles, be regarded as tasteless, ignorant and morally offensive.

There is, however, another vision of how love can be extended to more people – not because of their hidden virtues but because of their obvious shortcomings. It sounds deeply paradoxical at first: how could we be expected to love another person *because* they are awful?

To make better sense of this we can look at a series of works by the 17th-century Dutch artist Rembrandt van Rijn. Born in 1606, Rembrandt became a hugely successful painter when he was still only in his twenties. He earned a fortune and lived a wildly extravagant life.

But by his early fifties, he was all but bankrupt: he had to sell his house and all the beautiful objects he had accumulated. He only survived absolute penury thanks to the charity of his wife and son – whose financial situation he himself had made precarious. He never found a way back to prosperity and died a pauper in his early sixties. In the world of respectable, prudent Dutch merchants, such economic ruin was regarded as deeply shameful – and, self-evidently, it was his own fault. No one forced him to be a spendthrift; he'd been immensely

(Top) Rembrandt
van Rijn, *Rembrandt
and Saskia in the
Parable of the
Prodigal Son*,
c. 1635 (Bottom)
Rembrandt van
Rijn, *Self-portrait,
Aged 51*, c. 1657

fortunate, and he had wasted his opportunity. He was a well-known figure, and we can imagine how his contemporaries would have held him up as a model of a particularly awful type of person: a vain, greedy old fool.

Around the time financial disaster struck, Rembrandt painted a self-portrait, burdened with an honest, deeply sorrowful awareness of his own idiocy and folly: it is evident in his eyes that he knows he doesn't deserve anyone's sympathy.

Fittingly, given what he had gone through, his culminating masterpiece, painted at the very end of his life, relates to another, more famous character who has behaved appallingly.

The picture illustrates a parable from the New Testament known as the parable of the prodigal son. The kneeling man has been prodigal, in the sense of profligate: he took his father's money, ran away and spent it all on wine, women and music. He'd been brought up in a prosperous household, and had every advantage in life. And he's completely ruined it. The prodigal son stands in for Rembrandt himself – the waster who has brought ruin and disgrace upon himself. He has no claim on the kindness of anyone; he deserves to be hounded and humiliated. But this is not the reception he gets. In the painting, the elderly father figure greets his son with compassion and gentleness. Instead of giving his son the stern condemnation that he *deserves*, the

Rembrandt van Rijn, *The Return of the Prodigal Son*, c. 1668

father provides the love, warmth and forgiveness the son *needs*.

The picture conveys Rembrandt's moving and intimate realisation about the true nature of love: it reaches out to the selfish idiot, to the wastrel, to the passion-driven fool, to the person who has been granted so many good things and yet spoilt them. Love properly understood is destined also for the undeserving.

Perhaps Rembrandt's most moving work is a modest-looking print entitled *Christ Preaching*. Significantly, it isn't set in Galilee or Jerusalem in the 1st century CE. Instead, the message of kindness is being preached in a back street of a Dutch town – in other words, to Rembrandt's contemporaries.

The message can be boiled down to three words: 'I love you'. It is being conveyed to the kinds of people who in Rembrandt's day were viewed as particularly odious: thieves, layabouts, drunks, pimps and people who lent money at terrifying rates of interest; mean employers and con artists. They're not at all like Millet's honourable peasants;

Rembrandt van Rijn, *Christ Preaching*, c. 1652

they are not intended to be seen as remotely nice.
If Rembrandt were creating this work today,
we might see ranged around the alleyway the
representative unlovable figures of our times:
a politician who incites conflict, the owner of a
newspaper that puts profit above truth, someone
who is proud of their vulgarity, a snobbish socialite,
an arms trader, an aggressive youth, a sexual
deviant or the kind of person who takes satisfaction
in distressing others. It is to *them* that the message
of love is being directed.

Rembrandt's key insight was that he himself was a terrible person – not in all ways, but in some conspicuous and important ones. If he could turn out disastrously, so could anyone. If he needed redemptive forgiveness, so did everyone. What we might call the Rembrandt equation can be put like this: *I don't deserve love, but I need the love of others. Therefore, others who also don't deserve love will also need love – my love.*

Rembrandt wasn't asking people to tell him that what he had done was brilliant; he was clearly immensely irresponsible. His message of love doesn't say: *love me because I'm actually fine*; but rather: *despite the fact that I have done some terrible things, I still crave to be understood and viewed with tenderness and warmth.* In extending this kind of love to others, we're not suggesting they aren't scoundrels, criminals or menaces to civilisation. It's *because* they are that they need our compassion. And it is awareness of our own need for forgiveness that prompts us to extend forgiveness to them.

What holds us back from being more generous is often an unwillingness to see our own folly. It's true, of course, that we won't have done exactly what a conspicuously awful person has done. We may not, like Rembrandt, have brought financial ruin upon our family, but we have certainly done some stupid things. We may not have lied to the nation, but we have almost certainly lied to someone. We certainly haven't done every terrible thing, but we have done the central thing: we have hurt others. We may not have done so on a grand scale, but we've still done it. When we look at ourselves, as Rembrandt looked at himself, with honest shame, we begin to move to a recognition of the importance of a deeper and wider kind of love, the kind that embraces those who most need it: the unworthy.

A sense
of deprivation

What might most surprise and distress a visiting angel looking in on our species is just how many of us have hard hearts; that is, how many of us refuse to be moved by the sorrows of others. A sizeable majority will blithely mock those who have been disgraced, will celebrate someone's downfall, will spread devastating gossip about a neighbour, will join in on a round of online bullying and will look away while a former colleague is victimised. When wars break out or dictators take over, the evidence grows even darker: swathes of the population turn out to have an appetite for denunciation and betrayal, pogroms and massacres, public executions and show trials.

A big part of the explanation lies in a state of mind that perpetrators tend to be reluctant to own up to, because of how petty and undignified it can sound and how much of a vulnerability it reveals in their own characters: their hearts are cold because others have been cold to them in the past. They refuse to be loving because they don't see why they should be gentler and more generous towards others than others have been towards them. They feel they have so often been the victims of meanness, that they have no particular compunction about being mean in turn. When the moment comes, they spit on their neighbours as foes have previously spat on them. They kick as they have been kicked. They've had to face so many harsh realities, they don't see why others should be spared a dose of the punishments they have endured. Essentially what they are saying (though pride holds them back from actually saying it) is: *I can't love, because I haven't been loved.*

When we ask in vain 'But why could so many be so mean?' we miss the extent to which most people's lives are filled with a sufficient number of small moments of hurt, humiliation and suffering to render them ready to dig a knife into someone else when the occasion arises. The hurts and humiliations may be hard to discern, but they are present and profoundly influential nevertheless, and they add up. A bus route into work may be arduous, a knee might be sore, an apartment might be noisy and children disrespectful. When we try to get a job, maybe our applications are rudely rebuffed, our boss treats us with barely concealed contempt, people cut us up on the roads, we are rejected on dates, old friends we were at school with have successful businesses that put our careers to shame.

These may not sound like major incidents in and of themselves, but their cumulative impact can generate a powerful sense that the world is not a kind or tender place, that no one especially cares about us, that we are never honoured, protected or soothed, and that we therefore have no particular need to respond with generosity to anyone, let alone someone who has messed up their lives or acted unwisely in areas where we have shown restraint. Why wouldn't we say something sarcastic to a stranger online, given how tedious our journey to work is every morning? Why wouldn't we mock the adulterer, given how fractious and sexless our marriage is? Why wouldn't we celebrate the ruin of the once successful business person, given how little reward we have found in our jobs?

When attempting to explain the horrors witnessed in wars, there has been particular puzzlement as to how educated and relatively prosperous people end up committing the vilest deeds. How could university-educated people turn into killers? How could people who grew up in villas on leafy avenues emerge as police informers or torturers?

But this is to overlook how little the sense of deprivation that hardens people's hearts has to do with educational or financial lack, and how much it is emotional deprivation that renders us unable to love. It's possible for a person to be sent to the finest university and to read Goethe and Plato, Schiller and Descartes and still come out with a lust for vengeance because they had harsh and punishing parents or have been repeatedly rejected in love. There is enough ongoing suffering even in the lives of so-called 'privileged' people to explain why they too might join in with the mob or gleefully send old friends to the guillotine.

To start to create a more loving world has to involve an unfamiliar move: that of showing kindness and patience not just to those who have been the victims of meanness, but towards the mean themselves. We have to take on board the extent to which everyday meanness is the fruit of a long and slow series of everyday humiliations: the people who mock and slander, gossip and denounce have been hurt themselves in often unobvious ways that have left them with no kindness to spare. They may have some money and a decent enough job, but something has enraged and hurt them enough that they will be keen on vengeance and ready to stand by while strangers suffer.

A world that responds more lovingly at moments of crisis will require a broad acknowledgement of how much we hurt one another in unobtrusive ways – ways that end up calcifying our capacities for kindness.

It might help our collective levels of goodness and gentleness if people were more able to openly feel sorry for themselves for the sufferings they have undergone and so purge the buried resentments that fuel viciousness. Rather than being required to be brave and disguise feelings of hurt, we might admit that we are thoroughly fed up with how awful our relationships have been, how annoyed we are with our bosses, how sad we are that we aren't earning more money, how jealous we are about the success of strangers, and how angry we are with the ugliness of our cities.

In response to such woes – even if our house is relatively comfortable and our education was decent enough – we should be met with sympathy and understanding. Of course we are annoyed, of course it's tough that we aren't sufficiently rich, beautiful or successful, it's normal that we are maddened that we have been sidelined and ignored, that we aren't properly appreciated and that we will have to die with most of our potential untapped.

Once we have been fully allowed to scream and then been stroked and soothed, we may be in a better position to show kindness to strangers; we may be able to give a break to the prisoner or show forbearance to the felon. But until we have been properly and deeply indulged, it will be normal and predictable that we don't find it in ourselves to show mercy to our victims; the cruel are simply those to whom cruelty has too regularly been shown.

The feeling that as life is hard, we have to be hard too

Some of what holds people back from showing greater love is a sense that it would be dangerous and woolly-minded to do so. Too much sensitivity and sweetness, too much tolerance and sympathy appear to be the enemies of an appropriately grown-up and hard-headed existence. Such types are not saying that it wouldn't be delightful if we could display compassion and tenderness towards one another, if we could be sensitive to the sufferings of strangers and quick to forgive and understand the failings of our colleagues and lovers; they just don't think that this has much relevance in the real world.

In seeking to show why, they might refer to cases like that of the early 19th-century English poet John Keats, a gifted young man who wrote movingly about birds, the sky and autumn mists, and stands as a representative of a universal attitude of gentleness and kindness, an exemplar of sensitivity and love.

Joseph Severn, *John Keats*, c. 1821–1823

Keats' life was far from an inspiration, however; indeed, it was a practical disaster. He trained as a doctor, but never got a job; he received a modest inheritance on his mother's early death, but never managed to earn any money and was constantly pursued by creditors. His poems were not very well received; one particularly practical-minded reviewer, Thomas Carlyle, described him as 'a miserable creature', longing for 'a world of treacle', in which everyone and everything is sweet. He died of tuberculosis aged 25.

There seemed to have been a fatal misalignment in his life: Keats was broadly and warmly loving, but success eluded him. His ideas may have sounded elevated, but they didn't help him to secure health or peace of mind. If we are to thrive, the interpretation goes, we need to harden ourselves, be realistic and accept the painful but important fact that excesses of sensitivity and kindness actively ruin our chances of professionally flourishing.

Yet the temptation here is to assume that being loving and being realistic are contraries, that they are set like a fork in the road. We can be practical *or* we can be loving, but never both. The dispute is commonly translated in political terms; broadly, one side wants to be kind but will probably destroy the economy, the other side wants to support material prosperity, but the means will be brutal.

What has too often been missing in our ideas is the possibility that we might hold on to both love and rigour. Rather than seeing practicality and sympathy as alternatives, we could see them as different ingredients within a life. We're not being asked to choose; good results must depend on a combination.

An exclusively loving person might be inclined to overlook how much love needs a clear eye for unwelcome facts. It's not loving to tell someone that their business idea is bound to succeed when it is in fact naïve or unworkable. It's not loving to persuade someone that they are delightful just as they are when they may benefit from acquiring further skills or education. Love that loses touch with the reality of an imperfect world is no longer kind.

Yet the pure pragmatist, who trusts that cynicism lends them a perfect grip on how things work, is equally deluded. Kindness and generosity are essential lubricants; to get the best out of people involves magnanimity and decency; in order to negotiate successfully we need to feel the legitimacy of another person's concerns. If we are to persuade others of anything, we have to enter into their minds with solicitude.

We're lacking vivid descriptions and portrayals of people who have learned to be practical and loving. There have been too many people like Keats on the one hand and too many robber barons on the other. Sanity involves recognising that it is as naïve and ultimately as dangerous to surrender indiscriminately to the claims of love as it is to ignore them altogether.

The belief that people will only change when one is tough on them

One of the reasons why we might hold back from showing love is a belief that people only ever reform their ways when one treats them with harshness. It's by being handled toughly that wrongdoers finally see their errors; kindness is a fast route to laxness and recidivism.

It may sound sensible, but the truth, best observed from within our own lives, is that we tend to develop the strength to look inside ourselves and undertake the painful but necessary work of growth only when we feel broadly supported and sympathised with. It isn't partners who scream at us and tell us that we are silly who succeed in getting us to change our ways; it's those who show us enough forgiveness and mercy that we can dare to confront our failings. The same is true for issues of sexism or racism. No one has, it would seem, ever become a better person by being repeatedly called a damn fool or being slandered online by an army of enraged trolls.

We are creatures who evolve under the light of love. The fear is that if we love our enemies we'll be letting them off too easily. We should recognise that it is by refusing to offer them love that we ensure that they will continue to be exactly as they are.

The belief that
one doesn't have any
power to hurt

A lot of evil is done in the world by people who can't imagine that they have any power to hurt anyone. It's their sense that nothing is at stake in their behaviour towards others that leads them to ignore the rules of politeness and humanity and to kick people as if they were plated in armour.

In this respect they are paying homage to childhood. Think of the situation of a young child, of perhaps 6, who has fun mocking a parent's double chin or the wrinkles around their eyes. To this child, the parent is still, in many ways, an invulnerable deity. They live in a remote, impressive world of work, credit cards, driving and the news. How could someone of such stature be hurt by a comment about their less than perfect physique by a tiny person who can't spell properly?

But the child is missing the point. Their words do hurt. They can make their parents cry (in private). The child simply can't grasp how desperate and anxious their parent might be, how every morning they might stare in dismay into the bathroom mirror at the visible signs of ageing that speak to them relentlessly of a wrongly lived life. The parent, out of dignified generosity, has shielded their child from their own fragility. And now their child is paying them a beautiful, if misguided, compliment: a belief that they are beyond suffering.

Something related may happen when employees get together to gossip about the person they work for. In their imagination, the boss is so far above them that it couldn't possibly matter what they say about them. It's only when they themselves move to senior positions that they realise how vulnerable the person in charge might feel, how normal it is to want to be liked (even if you have a seat on the board) and how imperfect your self-esteem might be.

This idea casts a useful light on the activity of particularly dangerous people online. Their venom isn't the expression of a feeling of power. Rather, the troll tends to feel like a medieval vagabond outside a heavily fortified city, hurling insults and threats at what they take to be comfortable inhabitants sleeping behind metres of stone walls lined by vigilant troops. They want to hurt, but they don't imagine they actually can; that is what renders them so vicious.

True kindness may require us to take on board an unfamiliar idea: however young we are, however forgotten and ignored we feel, we have a power to cause other people serious damage. It isn't because we aren't wealthy or revered in elite circles that we lose a capacity either to comfort or to wound strangers. We become properly moral, and properly adult, when we understand that we may all ruin someone's day, and on occasion, through a few incautious and misplaced words, their life.

IV.
Conclusion: Towards a More Loving World

How nice people
should win

What has traditionally held the world back from becoming a more loving place is that those who are most effective at shaping practical life have tended to be least interested in promoting loving attitudes, whereas those most devoted to such attitudes have tended to lack the skills, confidence and temperament to alter the way their societies function. There has been a fateful divorce between noble aspirations on the one hand and executional strength on the other.

A thinker who reflected with unusual intensity on this division was the 16th-century Florentine political theorist and advisor Niccolò Machiavelli. His work pivots around a central, uncomfortable observation: that the wicked tend to win. And they do so because they have a huge advantage over the good: they are willing to act with the darkest ingenuity and cunning in the pursuit of their ends. They are not held back by those dastardly opponents of victory: principles. They are prepared to do anything to ensure that they get their way:

lie outright, twist facts, make threats or get violent. When the situation demands it, they will also seductively deceive, use charm and honeyed words, bedazzle and distract. They understand money and the law. They have access to influential figures. They grasp how prestige works. They can command teams. As a result, they are able to conquer the world.

By contrast, the good are hampered by their belief that the only requirement for being a good person is a warm heart. They trust that if one wants to create a more serious world, one can win people over through serious argument rather than clickbait. If one wants a fairer world, one can try to persuade the agents of injustice to surrender willingly rather than through intimidation. And if one wants people to be kind, one can show kindness to one's enemies rather than ruthlessness. In extremis, one can beg and implore, break down and appeal for mercy.

It may sound appropriate, but Machiavelli couldn't overlook an incontrovertible problem: it seldom works. As he looked back over the history of his native Florence and the Italian states more generally, he observed that the gentler and more loving princes, statesmen and merchants tended to meet miserable ends. It was this that drove him to write the short book for which we know him today, *The Prince*, a manual of advice for rulers about how not to finish last.

Machiavelli's core proposition is that, however noble and kind one's intentions, one should never be overly devoted to acting nicely when attempting to bring them about. Indeed, one has to borrow from every trick employed by the most cynical, dastardly and unscrupulous people ever to have lived: Nero, Caligula, Genghis Khan ...

Machiavelli knew where our counter-productive inclinations to act too nicely originated: the West was brought up on the Christian story of Jesus of Nazareth, the nice man from Galilee who always treated people well and wound up as the king of kings and the ruler of eternity. But Machiavelli pointed out an inconvenient aspect of this tale of the triumph of goodness through meekness. From a practical perspective, Jesus' life was a disaster. This gentle soul was trampled upon and humiliated, disregarded and mocked. Judged in his lifetime and outside of any divine assistance, he was one of history's greatest losers.

Machiavelli felt the clue to being effective lay in overcoming all vestiges of this story. *The Prince* is not a guide to being a tyrant, as is often thought; it is a guide as to what kind and loving people should learn from tyrants. It is a book about how to be effective rather than simply good. It is a book haunted by examples of the impotence of the decent.

The admirable prince – and today we might add, the CEO, political activist or thinker – should learn every lesson from the slickest, most devious operators who mould reality. They should know how to scare and intimidate, cajole and bully, entrap and beguile. The good politician needs to learn from the cynical one; the earnest entrepreneur from the oleaginous one. And those wanting to promote a more loving world should take inspiration from geniuses at selling bars of soap or annual gym subscriptions: they should challenge existing legislation, raise large sums of money, strongarm media outlets and take on bullies and mobs with savagery. They should not be intimidated by the resoluteness of those they oppose.

We are all ultimately the sum of what we achieve, not what we intend. If we care about love, or wisdom, kindness or virtue, but only ever act lovingly, wisely, kindly and virtuously, we may get nowhere. We may have to pick up ideas from unexpected sources, from those who appal us with their pugnacious manner. They have the most to teach us about how to bring about our wishes. We need weapons of similar grade steel to theirs.

It is not enough to dream well: the true measure is what we can get done. The goal is to change the world for the better, not reside in the quiet comforts of good aspirations. All this Machiavelli knew and urges us to take note of. He disturbs us for good reason, because he probes us where we are at our most self-serving. We tell ourselves that we didn't get there because we were a little too pure, good and kind. Machiavelli bracingly informs us that we are stuck because we have been too short-sighted to learn from the devils who know the secrets to bringing about the changes we yearn for.

Repetition

The greatest part of human unkindness has a banal but momentous source. It is rooted in our proclivity to forget. We do not set out to be mean, we have no vested interest in callousness, we are not committed to cruelty; at central moments, we simply *forget* our loving intentions. Our minds go elsewhere, we fall under different influences, something else crops up. The evils of the world unfold under the aegis of distraction.

There are beautiful selective moments when most of us are inflamed by a wish to be more loving people. If someone could peer into our hearts during such morally elevated instances, they would find unforeseen capacities for sacrifice, an inexhaustible empathy for the sufferings of strangers and a longing to spend the rest of one's days at the service of others.

Typically, such moods are aroused by works of art. After two hours spent watching a particular sort of film, we may come out of a cinema sure of the need to reorient our priorities. We tell ourselves that we'll no longer be blind to our selfishness, we'll take care to peer beneath the surface of our enemies' behaviour, we'll be patient and thoughtful; we'll make peace with our families and remind those we care for what they mean to us.

The influence of such a film is likely to be at its height in the period immediately after its screening. In the four hours after, we may approximate the valour of saints. Yet by the next morning, things will have started to go hazy. We will know that the film was profoundly affecting, but its details might escape us. By lunchtime, we'll struggle to summarise the plot. By the following weekend, it will be hard to remember we even saw it.

We aren't so much evil as congenitally absent-minded. The entities that best recognised this proclivity and worked assiduously to correct it were religions. One way to interpret their structure is to think of them as giant engines for remembering. They built armouries against our sieve-like minds. Between three and seven times a day, they asked us to get down on our knees and repeat an identical set of prayers. Once a week at least, they got us to reread a central passage of a holy book. They equipped our homes with icons and figurines so that we might look up from the washing up or the children's supper and catch the beseeching eyes of Mary or the imperturbable smile of the Buddha and remember to be graceful and calm, tolerant and forgiving.

They ensured that we were never far from works of art that could excite our moral sense; they employed the most emotionally affecting painters, sculptors and architects to make sure the ceilings were evocatively painted and the places of worship were filled with the right arches and coloured lights. They knew to be there at the central moments of life: at our birth, our wedding and our death. And as we surveyed the skyline of our villages and cities, it was their buildings that stood out in their majesty and scale. Forgetting was not an option.

We have been a great deal more careless in our handling of the ideas that supposedly matter to us most. We still venerate art, but we imbibe it in casual and unstructured ways. We make students read the important texts, but only once, over a few months before an exam, and then mistakenly assume that these lessons will stick for life. We don't remember anything by heart. We rarely watch films twice; it would feel bizarre to suggest we might rewatch some of them every month. It may have been decades since we were prompted to pick up poems whose ideas we are ostensibly committed to. We are recklessly negligent of our own best intentions.

We are instead obsessed with novelty, with encountering entirely unfamiliar concepts and works, as though our salvation depended on meeting with notions lacking any reference to what is already well known. Religions did not fall into this trap; they were unbothered by the surface obviousness of what they sought to tell us: *be kind, forgive, do not hold grudges, atone, look into their hearts, do not be cold* ... It didn't matter that this had been said a million times; this was only evidence of how important it was. They lacked the vanity to insist that their truths be new or abstruse. They didn't mind uttering their philosophies in the language of a child.

We have much to learn from these patient engines of repetition. We know what we need to do – the ideas are in us already – but we have allowed them to grow inert. At a collective and individual level we lack the right prompts to lead us back to the lives we aspire to.

It is little use allowing artists to follow their diverse whims and rewarding them with random prizes; as in the great days of religious art, we should commission artists to breathe life into already well-established principles, so that there might be multiple, intra-generational efforts to create the best portraits of love; the most affecting renditions of family harmony; the most inspiring visions of the majesty of kindness.

We should be directive about what our great monuments and public buildings are for. The priority is not for yet more museums loosely housing a scattering of distinguished art or concert venues able to accommodate a medley of events. As in the days of old, we need focused temples to kindness, cathedrals to forgiveness, monuments to goodness. If love remains our pilot light, we need to give it the sustenance and prominence we tell ourselves it deserves. We can't pretend that we will remember the ideas that will save us for more than a few hours. We need to insulate ourselves against the corruption of our weak memories. It is not enough to want to be kind; the challenge is to keep remembering the ardour with which we once wished to be so – three and a half long hours ago.

Censorship

Part of remaining kind means paying greater attention to the voices and influences we leave ourselves open to. We are over-optimistic on this score. We trust that we might be capable of flipping through the daily paper, scrolling through our feeds, taking in a slew of online comments, dropping into a succession of podcasts, and come away unaffected, with our hearts intact and our moral principles unaffected.

The German philosopher Hegel remarked that the world became modern when we replaced morning prayers with the newspaper; in other words, when we exchanged ten minutes of peaceful immersion in ideas of tolerance, tenderness and forgiveness for an encounter with a fast-moving stream of the world's greatest tragedies and sorrows narrated with prodigious (but almost invisible) macabreness and spite by a professional class commercially committed to exciting hatred, envy, fury and an inability to look away.

If we allow that our hearts can be raised and enhanced by a brief encounter with a beautiful poem or song, we have to be equally ready to admit the damage that might be caused by repeated contact with the callous and venomous tones of journalists and advertisers, pundits and trolls. We are more sensitive and endangered than we give ourselves credit for. If we allowed much of what we read and hear to resonate properly within us, we would need to take to bed for the day – or fairly lose our minds.

To stand any chance of maintaining our integrity, we need censorship. We have been taught by commercial interests masquerading as defenders of liberty to be scared of the word, associating it with the methods of repressive regimes. But there is another, far more natural and important kind of censorship, which involves keeping a close eye on the influences we allow into our orbit, so that we can maintain a hold on our own values and our serenity. Censorship doesn't have to mean being denied what one wants to hear; it can involve creating a silence so that what we know and love has the chance to assume the dimensions we long for it to have.

On any realistic time scale, we cannot hope to institute the collective elevated censorship our hearts require; to take down the advertising hoardings or ban the addictive algorithms. We need to do the work on our own, via conscious efforts to alter how our days start, what we check in the moments between meetings and what we consult last thing at night. We need to will ourselves to be a little unusual in our own era, to resist the pressures to be informed of much of what is, in reality, wholly unimportant; we should take pride that we aren't too much in the know, because we have finally learnt to keep what actually matters in mind.

A monastery

In the course of their thinking about love, religions eventually came to a surprising-sounding realisation: if we are to remain our best selves, given the conditions of the world, we may need to go to a monastery.

They chose sites, often of great natural beauty, on a hillside or clifftop, far from habitations, on which to build protected communities where members could devote themselves to peace and faith. Behind high walls, there were few distractions. One could work, socialise with and learn amongst people who were all equally committed to ideas of love. There weren't any divisions between one's career and personal life; one might spend a morning working in the kitchen or the gardens, and an afternoon in the library or on a meditative walk with a friend.

We should rightly feel how much we miss being in such places; how little peace we have, how jostled we perpetually are, how many people we have to spend time with who are unaligned with our values.

We may not be able to build ourselves actual secular monasteries (though we should try eventually), but we can right now assemble a mobile version of one in our minds. We can remind ourselves of the need to insulate ourselves from unfortunate influences, bring our work as much as possible into line with our principles, socialise only with people who can enhance rather than undermine our moods – and spend a good deal of every day in silence and reflection. To strangers, we may look entirely typical. In ourselves, we can have the comfort of knowing that we are able to retreat in our thoughts to the calm of a restorative hilltop cloister.

Rehabilitation

We often stay committed to nastiness because we are too invested in our ways to do anything else. It's been too long now since we have been in the camp of those who denigrate and condemn, who are cynical and mean-spirited. All our allegiances are to this embittered clan and we have burnt all bridges to other sorts.

But a loving world knows to leave a way back for people who wish to change their ways. There is no point speaking of love on the one hand and, on the other, denying people a chance to alter their course.

Kind parents know never to set the bar for confession too high nor to insist on too great a price for atonement. A child who has done something wrong needs every encouragement to feel that if they were to say sorry, they would swiftly be greeted warmly and accepted back into the fold.

Our vengeful, justice-focused world fails to understand the utility of forgiveness. It is keen to track down and condemn wrongdoing, but unused to offering people an amnesty or rewarding their honesty and desire to change. The mob is inflamed, rather than appeased, by an apology. Much of the time, saying sorry is a reckless strategy. There are perverse incentives to deny that one has ever done anything blameworthy. And because we are not trusted and permitted to change, we cannot confess that we ever erred.

We tell lies when we feel that our truths will be judged harshly, but our underlying hope is to cleanse ourselves. A loving world promises that it will be kind to those who are brave enough to admit when they have been unkind; it won't attach intolerable punishment to freely admitted errors.

Coda

It isn't easy to improve humanity, but we can make progress by realising where our problems lie: that it is a deficit of love that aggravates our most acute dilemmas and griefs.

We aren't used to speaking in emotional language about large-scale political matters. We analyse our wars and riots, our swagger and corruption, our fear and our paranoia through other lenses. We talk in terms of class and income differentials; we focus on educational scores and social capital. In plotting for better societies, we think of improving access to jobs and schools, of regulating stock markets and controlling the proliferation of weapons and polluting industries.

These are not unimportant priorities; it is just that if we search beneath them for what is truly at stake, we quickly come up against issues that more rightly belong to love: we are at war with ourselves and one another because we have not been sufficiently reassured. Our greed and our heedlessness are driven by fear and an unconscious memory of neglect. We are deranged, over-ambitious and furious because we have not been soothed in compassionate and serene arms. Our crimes spring from defensive terror and a sense of humiliation. We are unhappy bullies who pass on our injuries and our shame to those weaker than ourselves.

We have gone astray by limiting our discussions of love to the private realm. We need to reclaim this derided and debased word, endow it with maximal seriousness and reach, and use it to make sense of the greatest part of what is destroying us; love deserves to become our guiding term as we fumble our way towards the better, kinder world we yearn for.

Picture credits

Cover   Bart Jaillet / Unsplash

p. 17   Abraham Solomon, *First Class: The Meeting ... and at First Meeting Loved*, 1854. Oil on canvas, 69 cm × 97 cm. National Gallery of Canada, Ottawa, Canada / Wikimedia Commons

p. 20   Robert Altman / Michael Ochs Archives / Getty Images

p. 24l   Alexandros of Antioch, *Venus de Milo*, c. 130–100 BCE. Louvre Museum, Paris, France. Mattgirling / Wikimedia Commons (CC BY-SA 3.0)

p. 24b   Cosimo Rosselli, *Sermon on the Mount*, c. 1481–1482. Fresco, 349 cm × 570 cm. Sistine Chapel, Vatican, Rome, Italy. Granger Historical Picture Archive / Alamy Stock Photo

p. 26   Balthasar van Cortbemde, *The Good Samaritan*, 1647. Oil on canvas, 199.4 cm × 244.6 cm. Royal Museum of Fine Arts Antwerp, Antwerp, Belgium / Wikimedia Commons

p. 39   Bettmann / Getty Images

p. 94   John Constable, *Study of the Trunk of an
         Elm Tree*, c. 1821. Oil on paper, 30.6 cm ×
         24.8 cm. V&A Museum, London, England.
         Album / Alamy Stock Photo

p. 96   Johan Thomas Lundbye, *Study of Flowers
         and Plants*, 1840. Pen, black ink, brush
         and watercolour, 27.3 cm × 19.8 cm. Image
         courtesy of Statens Museum for Kunst

p. 97   Jakob Alt, *View from the Artist's Studio
         in Alservorstadt toward Dornbach*, 1836.
         Watercolor over pencil drawing on paper,
         52.1 cm × 42.1 cm. Albertina, Vienna,
         Austria / Wikimedia Commons

p. 102   Jean-François Millet, *The Angelus*, 1857–
         1859. Oil on canvas, 55 cm × 66 cm.
         Musée d'Orsay, Paris, France / Wikimedia
         Commons

p. 104t Rembrandt van Rijn, *Rembrandt and
         Saskia in the Parable of the Prodigal Son*,
         c. 1635. Oil on canvas, 161 cm × 130.5 cm.
         Gemäldegalerie Alte Meister, Dresden,
         Germany / Wikimedia Commons

p. 104b Rembrandt van Rijn, *Self-portrait, Aged 51*, c. 1657. Oil on canvas, 52.7 cm × 42.7 cm. National Gallery of Scotland, Edinburgh, Scotland. Ian G Dagnall / Alamy

p. 106 Rembrandt van Rijn, *The Return of the Prodigal Son*, c. 1668. Oil on canvas, 262 cm × 205 cm. Hermitage Museum, Saint Petersburg, Russia / Wikimedia Commons

p. 108 Rembrandt van Rijn, *Christ Preaching*, c. 1652. Etching and dry point, 15.4 cm × 20.7 cm. National Gallery of Art, Washington DC, USA / Wikimedia Commons

p. 118 Joseph Severn, *John Keats*, c. 1821–1823. Oil on canvas, 56.5 cm × 41.9 cm. National Portrait Gallery, London, England / Wikimedia Commons

On Failure

How to succeed at defeat

A reassuring guide on how to overcome failure, teaching us that we can learn to fail well.

This is a hopeful, consoling, gentle book about failure. Our societies talk a lot about success, but the reality is that no one gets through life without failing. Sometimes our failures are very obvious, at other times, we feel we have to conceal them out of shame. This book encourages us to accept the role that failure plays for all of us and to feel compassion for ourselves for the messes we can't help but make as we go through our lives.

It's a perfect volume for anyone who has ever had a relationship breakdown, suffered a career reversal, made enemies, bungled a project or wasted their time – in other words, for all of us.

ISBN: 978-1-912891-67-2
£15 | $19.99

The School of Life is a global organisation helping people lead more fulfilled lives. It is a resource for helping us understand ourselves, for improving our relationships, our careers and our social lives – as well as for helping us find calm and get more out of our leisure hours. We do this through films, workshops, books, apps, gifts and community. You can find us online, in stores and in welcoming spaces around the globe.

THESCHOOLOFLIFE.COM